ATTITUDE

The Path To Empowered Living

L E A P Learning Empowerment & Achieving Potential

ISBN 978-93-81115-71-8

First published in 2011 by Leadstart
A brand of One Point Six Technologies Private Limited
Unit no. 26, Ground Floor, A1, Shram Safalya,
Wadala Truck Terminal Road, Near Post Office,
Antop Hill, Mumbai -400037.
Email:info@leadstartcorp.com
www.leadstartcorp.com

Marketed & Distributed in India by Unbound Script
2/41, Ansari Road, Darayaganj, Delhi - 110002

EDITORS OF LEADSTART

The Editors of Leadstart are a team of passionate literary enthusiasts with a creative and progressive focus. Our team includes distinguished authors, researchers, contributors, in-house editors, and writing talent from around the world. Many literary projects require a diverse team rather than a single author to write or update the book. These projects often involve cases where the original author is unable to continue, whether because they are unavailable or no longer with us. Our work thus spans a range of content, from original writings to thoughtfully abridged classics, updated editions, and translations.

ABOUT THE LEAP SERIES

The LEAP series of books has been conceived as a tool of empowerment for every individual to achieve their full potential.

There are certain aspirations that every person in the world shares. We all want to be happy. We all want to lead fulfilling lives. We all want to find our soulmate. We all want a job we love doing. We all want good friends who will share our joy and sorrow. We all want to believe that there is a purpose to our lives.

While the commonality of these goals spans the globe, their achievement is entirely individual. Each person possesses a unique and mixed gift of strengths and weaknesses, special talents and handicaps. To focus our individual lives on all that is positive within us, all that is possible for us to do, to be and to achieve, we need to take conscious steps towards it. The empowerment of our lives is an individual pursuit. The decisions are yours. The action is yours. To do the very best with what one has been given – that is the ultimate achievement of a life well lived.

You Are You
First, we must recognise ourselves and accept our particular basket of capabilities. Nobody is the same. Nor is it necessary to be like someone else.

Find Your Horizons
Once we are at peace with the composition of our own individuality, we can set out to enhance our capabilities in order to achieve full potential as an individual. We can utilize all the teaching around us to stretch our talents to the fullest extent in order to achieve worthwhile goals.

Cap The Leak
Once we recognize our potential, we can work to minimize the influence and impact of our weak points in order to allow the strengths to shine in everything we do.

Row Your Boat
Every day is part of the journey. Sometimes you win the day. Sometimes the day is lost. But you keep rowing towards the shore, towards your goals. In India, it is called sadhana. That special power within you drives you to achieve what you have set yourself to do.

The **LEAP** series teaches methods of individual empowerment.

ൈ

CONTENTS

INTRODUCTION

Is the Glass Half Full or Half Empty?

A positive attitude is one of the most valuable qualities a person can cultivate. It influences how you interpret experiences, how you respond to challenges, and how you relate to the people around you. Having a positive attitude does not mean pretending that everything is perfect or ignoring the difficulties in life. It means choosing to meet those difficulties with clarity, courage, and the willingness to look for solutions. A positive attitude transforms ordinary moments into opportunities for learning and growth. It gives you the ability to see possibilities where others see only problems, and it allows you to move forward even when circumstances are not ideal.

Every person views the world through their own internal lens. Two individuals can face the same event and have entirely different experiences. One may see failure and frustration, while the other recognises a chance to learn something new. What separates the two is not luck or circumstance, but attitude. It is the quiet force that determines whether a challenge becomes a stepping stone or a stumbling block. When you train yourself to think constructively and act with intention, you discover that attitude is not something that happens to you; it is something you create.

This book is about understanding the creative power within yourself. It explores how your mindset shapes your behaviour, your health, and your overall quality of life. It offers simple ways to build awareness, strengthen emotional balance, and bring optimism into your daily routine. A positive attitude is not about ignoring pain; it is about working through it with perspective and strength. It teaches you to respond thoughtfully rather than react impulsively, to take responsibility instead of finding fault, and to direct your energy toward growth instead of complaint.

Attitude can be described as the sum of your thoughts, emotions, and habits expressed through your words and actions. It is visible in your posture, your tone of voice, and even your body language. It is the invisible atmosphere you bring into every situation. A positive attitude attracts cooperation, respect, and trust, while a negative one often creates resistance and tension. The encouraging truth is that attitude is learned behaviour. It can be improved and strengthened with awareness and practice, just as physical fitness improves with regular exercise.

Negativity often develops quietly. It begins with small frustrations or disappointments that we repeat to ourselves until they start to feel permanent. Over time, this creates a cycle of complaint and self-criticism that drains energy and blocks progress. Many people do not realise how much power these small, recurring thoughts have. The mind follows where attention goes. If your thoughts are habitually focused on what is missing or what has gone wrong, your emotions and actions will follow that path. Fortunately, the same principle works in the opposite direction. When you focus on gratitude, effort, and possibility, you build emotional strength. Optimism is not the denial of reality; it is the decision to give more importance to what helps you grow.

Choosing positivity requires awareness and practice, not perfection. You will still experience anger, disappointment, or sadness, but you will learn not to let these feelings control you. You will begin to see that frustration is temporary, that failure is information, and that patience is a form of strength. A positive person does not have fewer problems than others. They simply handle them differently. They approach life with the belief that every situation can be improved and that each setback can be used to build resilience.

The impact of attitude reaches far beyond the individual. Emotions are contagious. One person's outlook can change the atmosphere of an entire room. When you meet someone calm, confident, and kind, you feel it immediately. Their attitude encourages trust and cooperation. The same is true for negativity; it spreads quickly and drains the energy of everyone nearby. When you choose to act from a positive, grounded mindset, you contribute not only to your own well-being but also to the emotional balance of the people around you. In this sense, your attitude is a gift that can inspire, comfort, and uplift others.

Throughout this book, you will explore the structure of attitude and how it influences behaviour. You will learn how to redirect negative thinking, build daily habits that support positivity, and use self-talk as a tool for confidence and composure. Each chapter will help you understand how thoughts become actions and how repeated actions create long-term change. You will find practical advice, reflection exercises, and simple practices that can be applied immediately. Together, these lessons form a complete guide to living with greater purpose, self-awareness, and balance.

The key to transformation is consistency. Small daily choices make a larger difference than dramatic changes that cannot be sustained. You may not feel positive every moment, but every time you choose patience over irritation or gratitude over resentment, you strengthen the foundation of a new habit. Over time, this builds emotional resilience and self-trust. You will notice subtle improvements: calmer reactions, more constructive communication, and a greater sense of direction.

A positive attitude begins as a personal choice and grows into a way of life. It is both the cause and the result of self-respect. When you make it your goal to think clearly, speak kindly, and act intentionally, you reclaim control over your mood and your outcomes. This book will guide you through that process step by step, helping you develop not only a brighter outlook but a more stable and confident sense of self.

You do not need to feel optimistic before you begin. You only need to be willing to learn and to practise. The willingness to see things differently is enough to start. Each thought, each word, and each action that supports growth is a small movement toward a stronger, steadier version of yourself. Over time, these movements will shape your life in ways that are both visible and deeply felt.

As you move through the chapters ahead, remember that attitude is the compass that points you toward peace and progress. It may not remove every obstacle, but it will always guide you to meet each one with strength, clarity, and hope. The glass is not half full or half empty; it is refillable. You hold the power to fill it again and again with meaning, gratitude, and possibility.

࿇

LEAP Learning Empowerment & Achieving Potential

Decoding the Power Within: Understanding Attitude

1

WHAT EXACTLY IS ATTITUDE? THE FOUNDATION OF BEHAVIOUR

The word *attitude* is used so casually in everyday life that its meaning often becomes blurred. We hear people say, "He has such a positive attitude," or "Her attitude is terrible," but few stop to consider what the word truly represents. Is it just a mood? A personality trait? A pattern of behaviour? In truth, attitude is a complex combination of thoughts, feelings, and actions that work together to shape how we respond to the world. It is both internal and external, both mental and behavioural, both learned and chosen.

An attitude begins as a thought, as a mental interpretation of something we encounter. That thought then triggers an emotional response, which finally influences how we act. For example, if you believe that a challenge is an opportunity to learn, you will likely feel motivated and behave confidently. But if you view the same challenge as a threat, your body may tense, your mind may resist, and your behaviour may become defensive or avoidant. The process happens so quickly that we often mistake the behaviour for instinct, when in fact, it is the visible outcome of an invisible pattern of thinking and feeling.

Psychologist Carl Jung described attitude as the "readiness of the psyche to act or react in a certain way." This readiness, the mental and emotional posture you adopt toward life, determines not only what you see, but how you interpret what you see. It shapes your perception of others, your sense of fairness, your tolerance for stress, and your expectations of yourself. Attitude is not simply what you think of the world; it is the lens through which you see and engage with it.

Broadly, attitudes can be grouped into three types: positive, negative, and neutral. A positive attitude is hopeful, resilient, and proactive. It seeks possibilities and focuses on progress rather than problems. A negative attitude, on the other hand, tends to emphasise limitations, past failures, or potential risks. It easily slips into blame, complaint, or doubt. A neutral attitude sits somewhere in between, calm, observant, and detached, yet not necessarily optimistic or pessimistic. Most of us shift between all three depending on circumstances, mood, and stress. It is even possible to experience positive and negative feelings simultaneously, such as feeling both nervous and excited before a new opportunity. The key is awareness: recognising where your mind naturally gravitates and learning how to guide it toward balance and growth.

Our attitudes are shaped by many influences, both internal and external. Family upbringing, culture, education, and social environment all leave their mark. So do intelligence, self-esteem, and emotional maturity. Experiences of trust or betrayal, success or failure, encouragement or rejection gradually form the mental framework through which we interpret new events. Even seemingly unrelated factors such as physical health, mood, and energy levels can alter how we perceive the world in a given moment. A person who feels well-rested and appreciated is more likely to react with patience, while someone who is exhausted or anxious may respond with irritation. Over time, these repeated responses crystallise into habits, and those habits become an attitude.

Human beings are naturally inclined to form attitudes because they help us make sense of a complex world. From an evolutionary perspective, quick judgments about safety, threat, or reward helped our ancestors survive. Those instincts still influence how we react today, even though the "dangers" are now more emotional or social than physical. When we feel ignored, criticised, or uncertain, our brains activate the same survival mechanisms that once protected us from predators. This is why anger, defensiveness, or withdrawal often appear before we have had a chance to think things through. The modern challenge is to use our awareness to pause before reacting, to question whether our instinctive response truly serves our current reality.

Persuasion, communication, and social influence also play powerful roles in shaping attitude. The messages we receive from peers, media, or authority figures can strengthen or undermine our beliefs. For example, a trusted mentor's encouragement can inspire confidence, while repeated exposure to cynical or fearful thinking can foster pessimism. In a world overflowing with opinions, maintaining a healthy attitude requires discernment, the ability to separate information that uplifts from that which diminishes. The source of a message matters as much as the message itself. Credibility, intent, and honesty influence how deeply words take root in our minds.

Another crucial insight is that attitude is not fixed. It evolves with awareness, learning, and deliberate choice. Just as muscles grow with exercise, positive attitudes strengthen with practice. Every time you choose patience over anger, curiosity over judgment, or gratitude over complaint, you reinforce new pathways in your brain. Over time, this repetition transforms temporary reactions into stable traits. The ability to choose your attitude, to consciously decide how you will think and behave, is one of the most powerful forms of freedom you possess.

Unlike instinct, which is automatic, attitude involves choice. It is the expression of your values, your maturity, and your willpower. You can decide to approach a setback with frustration or with determination. You can interpret criticism as an attack or as an opportunity to improve. Each decision creates a small shift in how you experience life. As these choices accumulate, they define your overall direction. A positive attitude, therefore, is not just a personal preference; it is a discipline that determines how effectively you live and work.

To summarise, attitude is not something you are born with; it is something you build. It reflects the combination of your thoughts, emotions, and actions; your personal signature on how you experience the world. It is shaped by many forces, but it is ultimately yours to direct. Once you understand that, you gain the power to reshape not just your mood, but your entire approach to life.

ጀወ

2

THE CLEAR ADVANTAGE

Why a Positive Attitude Is Better

Having a positive attitude is more than just "thinking happy thoughts." It is a way of seeing life that opens doors, builds resilience, and strengthens both your mind and body. When you adopt a positive attitude, you start to approach challenges as opportunities instead of threats. You begin to expect growth instead of failure. You become the kind of person who looks at the glass and says, "There is enough here to make something worthwhile." This mindset creates momentum. It energises you, sharpens your focus, and makes you more open to learning and connection.

A positive attitude does not ignore reality or deny that problems exist. Instead, it helps you face them with greater calm and confidence. When difficulties arise, positive thinkers ask, "What can I learn from this?" rather than "Why is this happening to me?" That small shift in language changes everything. It moves you from helplessness to purpose. Optimism gives you the strength to look beyond the current moment and to believe that improvement is possible, even when progress is slow. This belief fuels motivation, and motivation drives action.

On the other hand, a negative attitude can quietly limit your potential. It makes the glass look half-empty even when there is plenty to appreciate. Negativity tends to focus on what is missing or what might go wrong. It thrives on fear and self-doubt. Over time, this pattern of thinking weakens confidence and turns effort into hesitation. People who habitually think negatively often talk themselves out of taking action because they assume failure is inevitable. Their imagination, instead of being a tool for creativity, becomes a tool for worry.

A negative attitude can also create a cycle of low energy and poor health. When the mind constantly anticipates stress or disappointment, the body reacts as if those threats are real. Stress hormones rise, sleep becomes restless, and concentration declines. Over time, this mental strain affects physical well-being. The opposite is equally true. Positive thoughts encourage the release of chemicals like dopamine and serotonin, which improve mood, increase alertness, and enhance overall vitality. The mind and body work together. When one improves, the other follows.

Neutral attitudes, while less harmful than negative ones, also hold you back. A neutral mindset often shows up as indifference, not expecting much, not caring much, and not striving much. It might protect you from disappointment, but it also blocks enthusiasm. A neutral attitude says, "I'll wait and see what happens," instead of "I'll see what I can make happen." Life feels flat when you are not emotionally invested in your goals. Choosing a positive attitude requires more effort, but it also delivers far greater rewards.

Peer pressure and social influence can affect how easily you maintain positivity. It is common to worry about how others perceive you or to feel pulled toward group negativity. People who constantly complain or criticise can drain your energy without you realising it. That is why surrounding yourself with people who uplift you is so important. When you stop measuring your worth by others' opinions, you gain freedom. You no longer live for approval; you live from conviction. This independence strengthens confidence and gives your positivity a solid foundation.

The link between attitude and well-being is supported by both psychology and medicine. Researchers have found that optimistic people tend to have stronger immune systems, better cardiovascular health, and lower levels of stress-related illness. Their recovery from setbacks, both emotional and physical, is faster because they expect healing and improvement. In contrast, chronic negativity often leads to fatigue, headaches, and an increased sense of helplessness. The way you think shapes not only your mood but also your body's ability to function and recover.

Positive thinking also improves performance in everyday life. It helps you stay focused, creative, and adaptable. When you believe that effort leads to improvement, you become more willing to try new things. You take constructive feedback without feeling personally attacked, and you recover quickly from mistakes. These qualities make you more effective at work, more patient in relationships, and more persistent in achieving personal goals. A positive mindset is not about ignoring difficulties but about approaching them with curiosity and courage instead of fear.

Of course, nobody can stay positive all the time. There will be moments of frustration or disappointment. The goal is not perfection, but consistency. You can still acknowledge sadness, anger, or worry while maintaining a hopeful outlook. A balanced positive attitude is realistic, not naive. It accepts challenges without surrendering to them. The true strength of positivity lies in its flexibility, the ability to bend without breaking, to pause without quitting, and to see value even in struggle.

Building this attitude takes practice. It begins with awareness of your internal dialogue. Notice how you talk to yourself in moments of stress. Are your thoughts critical, doubtful, or defensive? Replace them with supportive statements such as "I can handle this," or "I've faced worse and grown from it." These small shifts gradually rewire your mental habits. Over time, you will find that your first response to challenges becomes calmer, your energy steadier, and your outlook more confident.

Ultimately, positivity is not about pretending everything is fine. It is about believing you have the capacity to make things better. It empowers you to act, to try, and to keep learning. The clear advantage of a positive attitude is that it works for you instead of against you. It strengthens your health, deepens your relationships, and opens your mind to the possibilities that negativity would otherwise conceal. When you choose to see the good, you create more of it.

ꕤ

3

POSITIVITY

More Than Just a Way of Thinking

Positivity is often misunderstood as simple optimism or cheerful thinking. Many people treat it as a surface-level quality, as if smiling more or saying the right words could instantly change everything. In truth, positivity is much deeper. It is not just a pleasant thought but a pattern of perception and behaviour that begins in the mind and spreads into every area of life. It starts quietly, with the way you interpret what happens around you, and gradually transforms how you act, speak, and relate to others.

Every positive habit begins with a single thought. Thoughts create emotions, emotions influence actions, and repeated actions form habits. Those habits, over time, shape who we become. This is the real power of positivity: it turns invisible thoughts into tangible outcomes. If your mind focuses on progress and solutions, your behaviour will naturally reflect persistence and openness. But if your inner dialogue is filled with self-criticism or fear, those emotions will eventually show up in your words, choices, and relationships. What you think repeatedly becomes what you live.

Developing positivity begins with self-awareness. Ask yourself two simple but revealing questions: How do I see myself? And how do others see me? These questions can expose a gap between how you perceive your abilities and how they are actually expressed in the world. You might see yourself as capable but hesitant, or strong but easily discouraged. Closing this gap requires honesty and practice. It means recognising that your inner narrative shapes your outer reality. If you speak to yourself with encouragement, you build confidence. If you allow the inner critic to dominate, you reinforce limitation.

Many people carry a habit of negative self-talk without realising it. They replay old mistakes, criticise themselves for imperfections, and assume they are not enough. This constant internal noise drains motivation and weakens the will to try. To reverse that pattern, you must consciously replace those thoughts with affirmations that strengthen rather than weaken. Instead of saying, "I am not ready," say, "I am learning and improving." Instead of thinking, "I always fail," remind yourself, "Every attempt brings me closer to success." This shift may feel small, but over time, it creates a completely different emotional atmosphere within you.

Positivity also requires imagination. You need to be able to picture yourself succeeding before success arrives. Visualisation is not daydreaming; it is mental preparation. When you consistently imagine yourself handling challenges calmly and achieving your goals, your mind becomes more confident and familiar with that version of reality. You begin to act in ways that make it possible. Athletes, musicians, and leaders across the world use this technique because it strengthens focus and removes unnecessary fear. When you can see the outcome clearly, you are far more likely to reach it.

At its core, positivity is not denial of hardship but belief in potential. It allows you to recognise difficulty without being defeated by it. Life will always bring challenges, but a positive mindset gives you the resilience to respond rather than react. It helps you pause, breathe, and ask, "What can I do next?" instead of, "Why is this happening to me?" This approach makes you adaptable. It turns obstacles into lessons, criticism into feedback, and failure into a temporary pause instead of an ending. With this mindset, even setbacks become part of progress.

Positivity is also relational. The way you treat yourself influences how you treat others. When you view life through a generous, open perspective, you naturally extend that kindness outward. You become more patient, more understanding, and more willing to listen. People are drawn to that energy because it makes them feel safe and inspired. Your positive attitude becomes a quiet example, showing others that calm confidence is possible even in uncertainty. This ripple effect strengthens not just your own emotional well-being but the atmosphere around you.

The journey toward a positive mindset is gradual. It takes time, repetition, and trust. You will not always feel upbeat or motivated, but consistency matters more than perfection. Each time you challenge a negative thought, each time you choose gratitude over complaint, you are training your mind to move in a new direction. Eventually, this practice becomes automatic. You start to see opportunities in difficulty, hope in change, and light even in moments of confusion.

To be truly positive is to be realistic, grounded, and hopeful all at once. It means believing that while you cannot always control events, you can always control your response. You can decide to face the world with curiosity instead of fear, determination instead of doubt. Over time, this choice builds emotional stability and deep self-respect. You begin to trust yourself to handle whatever comes next, and that trust becomes the foundation for lasting confidence and peace.

Positivity, therefore, is not just a way of thinking. It is a way of living that grows stronger each time you practise it. When your thoughts support your goals and your words align with your values, your actions begin to flow naturally toward growth and fulfilment. You start to experience life not as something that happens to you, but as something you actively shape.

ꙮ

4

THE IMMENSE POWER OF A POSITIVE ATTITUDE

Hugh Downs once said, "A happy person is not a person in a certain set of circumstances, but rather a person with a certain set of attitudes." This simple statement holds great truth. Happiness, contentment, and success rarely depend on perfect conditions. They depend instead on how we choose to interpret and respond to the conditions we face. Every thought you think, every word you speak, and every choice you make builds the framework of your attitude. Over time, this framework determines the quality of your life.

Your attitude shapes how you handle stress, disappointment, and conflict. It influences how you treat others, how you make decisions, and how you see yourself. When you maintain a positive attitude, you are better equipped to meet challenges with patience and creativity instead of frustration or fear. You become more resilient, more open to feedback, and more willing to adapt. What begins as a single decision to stay optimistic can eventually transform how you experience every part of life, both personal and professional.

Our thoughts are powerful because they do not remain only in the mind. They influence our emotions and, through them, our physical health. Scientific research supports this connection. Positive thinking encourages the body to release beneficial hormones, stabilise blood pressure, and improve immune response. It enhances focus, stamina, and even problem-solving ability. When your mind believes that progress is possible, your body responds with renewed energy and vitality. This interaction between thought and physiology is proof that positivity is not merely emotional—it is biological.

A positive attitude has the remarkable ability to change self-doubt into confidence. It shifts the focus from what might go wrong to what can be done right. When faced with obstacles, positive thinkers do not wait for perfect conditions. They act with courage and find value in learning through experience. This mental flexibility allows them to adapt quickly and maintain motivation even when progress is slow. With a positive attitude, you stop being a passive observer of life and become an active participant who shapes outcomes rather than fears them.

It is important to understand that a positive attitude does not mean ignoring difficulties or pretending that pain does not exist. Instead, it is about choosing a perspective that helps you move forward. Every challenge carries within it a lesson or an opportunity. The task is to look for that meaning rather than focusing solely on the hardship. This approach builds emotional strength. Over time, it helps you face uncertainty with calm and purpose.

The impact of a positive attitude extends into every area of your life. In your personal relationships, it fosters patience, understanding, and mutual respect. It allows you to listen more attentively and to respond with kindness instead of defensiveness. In professional life, it inspires collaboration and creativity. People naturally gravitate toward those who radiate optimism because they feel encouraged and supported in their presence. A positive person becomes a quiet source of motivation for others simply by example.

When positivity becomes a habit, several benefits begin to unfold. You develop stronger self-belief and an inner sense of stability that is not easily shaken by circumstances. You find that energy and enthusiasm come more naturally, even on difficult days. Your capacity for patience and perseverance grows. You begin to face fewer obstacles, not because life becomes easier, but because you approach problems with greater clarity and flexibility. Your mind opens to new ideas, and your confidence helps others trust and respect you in turn.

A positive attitude also enhances your ability to make sound decisions. Negativity clouds judgment and magnifies fear, while optimism encourages balanced thinking. When you believe that a solution exists, you are more likely to find it. Positivity does not eliminate obstacles, but it changes your relationship with them. Instead of feeling trapped, you feel challenged. Instead of being discouraged, you feel determined. This change in mindset often leads to outcomes that once seemed out of reach.

Ultimately, a positive attitude gives you control. It allows you to steer your emotions, manage your reactions, and choose the meaning you assign to your experiences. Life will continue to present moments of uncertainty, but with a steady and optimistic outlook, those moments no longer feel like threats. They become opportunities to grow, to strengthen your will, and to refine your character. Every time you respond positively, you reinforce your ability to live with confidence and joy.

The power of a positive attitude lies not in denying reality but in reshaping it. It begins quietly within the mind and then expands outward, influencing your words, your relationships, your health, and your achievements. When you cultivate this mindset, you begin to discover that happiness, strength, and peace of mind are not distant goals. They are natural results of how you choose to think today.

ꕤ

LEAP Learning Empowerment & Achieving Potential

Building the Positive Core: Habits, Focus, and Goals

5

TEN ESSENTIAL TIPS TO IGNITE YOUR POSITIVE JOURNEY

Staying positive is not something that happens overnight. It is a gradual process that requires intention, consistency, and a willingness to practice new ways of thinking. The good news is that positivity can be learned. With the right habits, you can train your mind to naturally focus on what uplifts you rather than what holds you back. Here are ten powerful approaches that can help you build and sustain a positive outlook, so that optimism eventually becomes your second nature.

1. **Accentuate the Good Things in Life**

   The first step is to accentuate the good things in life. Gratitude is one of the simplest and most effective ways to cultivate positivity. When you pause to acknowledge what is going well, you remind yourself that there is always something to appreciate, no matter how small. It could be a caring family, a loyal friend, or even a skill you take for granted. By focusing on what you already have rather than what you lack, you shift your mindset from scarcity to abundance. Over time, this practice strengthens self-worth and promotes a steady sense of contentment.

2. **Choose Words that Uplift and Empower**

   Next, choose the right words, because language shapes perception. The words you use in daily conversation reflect your inner thoughts and, in turn, influence your emotions. Building a positive vocabulary can change the way you experience life. Replace phrases such as "I can't handle this" with "I'm learning to manage this better." Speak with excitement and possibility. Words like "growth," "opportunity," and "joy" signal confidence and hope, while words like "failure," "impossible," or "worried" reinforce fear. What you repeatedly say becomes what you repeatedly believe.

3. **Surround Yourself with Positive Influences**

   Surrounding yourself with positive influences is equally important. People's energy is contagious, and the company you keep affects your attitude more than you might realise. Spend time with those who inspire, encourage, and uplift you. Limit exposure to constant criticism or negativity, as it can slowly drain motivation. Being in a supportive environment strengthens your emotional resilience, allowing you to remain optimistic even when circumstances are difficult. Seek out mentors, colleagues, and friends who challenge you to grow without diminishing your confidence.

4. **Focus on Your Strengths**

   To stay motivated, focus on your strengths. Everyone has a unique combination of talents and abilities that serve as their foundation for success. One practical way to discover them is to make two lists: one of the things you enjoy doing and another of the things you do well. The overlap between the two reveals your core strengths. When you work from these strengths, you naturally feel more confident and productive. Success in those areas reinforces a positive self-image, which in turn fuels more success—a cycle that builds self-belief over time.

5. **Let Go of the Past**

   Part of cultivating positivity is also learning to let go of the past. Holding on to regret, guilt, or resentment weighs down your mind and prevents you from experiencing joy in the present. The past cannot be changed, but it can be understood and released. Learn from it, forgive where necessary, and focus on what can be done now. When you stop replaying old memories of disappointment, you create space for new experiences and healthier perspectives to emerge.

6. **Celebrate Your Victories**

   Another important step is to celebrate your victories. Too often, we move from one goal to the next without pausing to acknowledge what we have achieved. Whether it is finishing a project, developing a habit, or simply getting through a tough week, every win deserves recognition. Celebration reinforces motivation. It reminds you that your efforts are paying off and that progress, no matter how small, is worth appreciating. When you honour your accomplishments, you condition your mind to look for success rather than failure.

7. **Face Problems with Courage and Clarity**

   A positive mindset also means having the courage to tackle problems head-on. Avoiding difficulties only allows them to grow larger in your imagination. Instead, train yourself to confront them calmly and constructively. Every problem has a solution, even if it takes time to find. Once you decide on a course of action, commit to it and move forward without overthinking. This kind of decisiveness builds inner strength and reduces the anxiety that comes from uncertainty. Confidence grows when you realise that you are capable of handling whatever comes your way.

8. **Find Joy in Play and Laughter**

   Amid the seriousness of goals and challenges, do not forget to have fun. Laughter and play are powerful tools for maintaining emotional balance. They remind you not to take life or yourself too seriously. A sense of humour can transform tension into connection and failure into perspective. Find moments of lightness every day: listen to music, share a joke, or revisit something that made your younger self happy. Fun recharges your energy, keeps your spirit agile, and helps you return to your work with renewed enthusiasm.

9. **Share Your Positivity with Others**

   Positivity multiplies when you share it with others. One of the most fulfilling ways to strengthen your own optimism is to lift others. Perform acts of kindness, whether it is helping a neighbour, volunteering, mentoring someone, or simply offering encouragement, and create a ripple effect that spreads far beyond your initial gesture. Giving your time and attention reminds you that you have value to offer. It connects you to others in meaningful ways and reinforces your sense of purpose.

10. **Let Love Guide Your Attitude**

    Finally, the deepest and most transformative source of positivity is love. Love for life, love for others, and love for yourself form the emotional core of lasting happiness. To love is to care, to forgive, to nurture, and to accept. It fills your days with meaning and keeps bitterness at bay. Make it a habit to express affection and appreciation to those you care about. Equally, treat yourself with the same kindness you would offer a close friend. When love becomes the foundation of your attitude, it softens your outlook and fills your interactions with warmth.

Developing positivity is not about forcing a smile or pretending that everything is fine. It is about creating a balanced mindset that values gratitude, courage, and compassion. Each of these ten habits works together to reshape your thought patterns and strengthen your emotional core. The more consistently you apply them, the more naturally optimism will guide your actions. Eventually, positivity will stop being a conscious effort and become an effortless way of being, one that fills your life with energy, confidence, and joy.

6

THE ART OF STAYING FOCUSED ON YOUR PATH

Focus is one of the greatest assets you can cultivate on your journey toward a positive and fulfilling life. It is the quiet force that bridges the gap between intention and achievement. In a world full of distractions, maintaining focus is not always easy. Our attention is constantly being pulled in different directions by noise, technology, obligations, and expectations. Yet, focus is what allows you to turn energy into progress. Without it, even the best plans remain unrealised.

When you choose to adopt a positive attitude, staying focused becomes easier because your thoughts and actions start to align. Positivity brings clarity. It helps you see beyond temporary setbacks and stay centred on what truly matters. Focus, then, is not just about discipline but also about direction. It is the ability to keep your mind steady on your goals while filtering out distractions that do not serve your growth. It is the art of saying no to what is trivial so you can say yes to what is meaningful.

One of the most effective ways to protect your focus is to be intentional about your environment. The people around you play a powerful role in either strengthening or weakening your determination. Surround yourself with individuals who believe in growth, who encourage you to do your best, and who celebrate your progress. Their optimism and drive will naturally lift your own. At the same time, distance yourself from those who constantly criticise or complain. Negative energy can easily seep into your thinking, clouding your judgment and slowing your progress. Protecting your mental space is not selfish but essential.

Staying focused also means letting go of distractions from the past. Regret and guilt are mental traps that can quietly drain your energy. While it is important to learn from mistakes, it is even more important to move beyond them. The past cannot be changed, but it can be understood and released. Every experience, good or bad, teaches something valuable. The moment you decide to let go of what no longer serves you, you reclaim the energy that can now be used to build your future. Focus is not only about what you look at. It is also about what you stop looking back at.

Living in the present moment is the most powerful way to stay on track. The present is where effort turns into action and action turns into results. Worrying about what might happen tomorrow or dwelling on what went wrong yesterday only divides your attention. Concentrate instead on what you can do today. Whether it is a small task or a major step toward your dream, do it with full attention. Consistency in small actions builds momentum. Over time, these efforts accumulate into remarkable achievements.

To remain focused, it is also important to cultivate emotional steadiness. A positive attitude helps you stay calm when faced with pressure. Instead of reacting impulsively to challenges, you learn to pause, breathe, and respond with clarity. This ability to stay composed keeps your mind from scattering when stress arises. Focus thrives in calmness. The more centred you are emotionally, the better you can channel your thoughts toward purposeful action.

Creating routines can also strengthen focus. Simple habits such as planning your day, setting priorities, and managing time effectively create a structure that supports concentration. When your daily life follows a clear rhythm, your mind does not waste energy on unnecessary decisions. It becomes easier to dedicate attention to what truly matters. Balance your work with rest, and remember to celebrate small victories along the way. Recognition of progress fuels motivation to keep going.

Finally, remember that focus grows stronger when it is tied to purpose. Ask yourself why you are doing what you are doing. When your goals align with your values, commitment feels natural. You no longer have to force concentration; it becomes the natural outcome of meaningful work. A person who knows their purpose is rarely distracted because they have already chosen what deserves their time and heart.

Focus is not about rigidly avoiding change but about guiding your energy wisely. It allows you to move with intention instead of drifting through life. Every decision, every thought, and every small act performed with awareness brings you closer to your vision. Stay patient with yourself as you practise this art. Some days your focus will waver, and that is normal. What matters most is returning to your path each time you stray, knowing that every step you take in the right direction builds the foundation for your success.

ꟷ

7

TACKLING NEGATIVITY

Reclaiming Your Inner Space

Negativity can quietly take root in our lives without us even realising it. It often begins with small, harmless thoughts, a complaint here, a judgment there, but before long, it becomes a pattern of seeing the world through a clouded lens. It feels easier to be negative than positive because complaining, criticising, and finding fault require less effort than practising patience, gratitude, or forgiveness. However, living in a constant state of negativity slowly erodes your emotional strength. It drains energy, clouds judgment, and leaves very little room for growth or happiness.

Many of us fall into this pattern because negativity offers a strange sense of comfort. It allows us to blame circumstances, people, or luck instead of taking responsibility for our emotions and actions. This avoidance can create a loop where complaining replaces effort and excuses take the place of accountability. Over time, the mind becomes conditioned to focus on what is wrong rather than what is possible. Breaking free from this cycle begins with awareness. You cannot change what you do not first recognise.

The first step toward reclaiming your inner space is to stop feeding the cycle of negativity. This means consciously halting the habits that reinforce it—criticism, blame, and self-doubt. Criticising others may feel momentarily satisfying, but it shifts focus away from self-improvement. Blaming others for your failures keeps you from learning from experience. Having low expectations of yourself limits your ability to grow. To reverse this mindset, make a conscious decision to focus inward. Ask yourself what you can do to improve, what you can learn, and how you can respond differently the next time. True empowerment begins when you realise that the power to change your life rests entirely within you.

It is impossible to maintain a positive outlook if you are perpetually unhappy, angry, or resentful. These emotions are signals that something within you needs attention. Take time to examine what is causing them. Are you holding on to disappointment, unresolved anger, or guilt? Write down the situations, people, or beliefs that make you feel unhappy or frustrated. Then, prioritise this list, starting with what troubles you the most. The act of writing gives your emotions shape and makes them easier to address. Once you have identified what weighs you down, begin working through it one step at a time. Some issues may resolve quickly, while others might require patience and persistence. Change is rarely easy, but it always begins with a single decision to take back control.

As you work to release negativity, you may encounter resistance from others or even from your own inner critic. Some people might mock your optimism or doubt your sincerity. Others might feel threatened when you begin to change because your growth challenges their comfort zone. Stay firm in your commitment. Remember that this process is not about pleasing anyone else; it is about freeing your own mind. Negativity thrives on reaction. When you stop engaging with it, it loses power over you.

One of the most powerful tools for overcoming negativity is the practice of positive affirmation. Affirmations are simple, constructive statements that help you reprogram your subconscious mind. Every day, countless thoughts pass through your mind, and research shows that most of them tend to be negative or repetitive. By consciously introducing positive affirmations, you begin to shift this internal dialogue. These statements serve as reminders of your potential, worth, and capacity for joy. Over time, they shape not just your thoughts but also your emotions and actions.

Start small and be consistent. Choose statements that resonate deeply with you, such as "I am happy," "I am capable," "I am surrounded by love," or "I have a healthy mind and body." Speak them aloud with confidence and sincerity, preferably in front of a mirror. The more you repeat them, the more your subconscious begins to accept them as truth. Use present-tense language that reflects who you are becoming, not who you were. Avoid negative phrasing such as "I will not be sad," and replace it with "I am at peace." Over time, these affirmations become internal truths that guide your behaviour and shape your reality.

Repetition is the foundation of transformation. Just as negative thinking can become a habit, so can positive thinking. Each time you choose to affirm something uplifting about yourself, you are rewiring your brain to look for evidence of that truth in your daily life. This creates a reinforcing cycle of confidence and contentment. The shift may not happen overnight, but it is steady and lasting. Eventually, positivity becomes your natural response rather than something you must force.

As your perspective changes, so will your interactions with the world. You will begin to smile more often, laugh more freely, and appreciate both yourself and others with genuine warmth. Small acts, such as expressing gratitude, complimenting someone, or spending time doing what you love, will amplify this feeling. These gestures may seem minor, but they have a profound cumulative effect on your mental state. Joy attracts joy, and once you open your mind to it, it multiplies effortlessly.

Reclaiming your inner space is not about pretending life is perfect; it is about recognising that peace and positivity are choices you can make each day. When you take responsibility for your emotions, use affirmations to redirect your thoughts, and act with kindness toward yourself, you begin to create a life that feels lighter and more fulfilling. The journey toward positivity is one of continuous self-awareness and self-compassion. Each moment offers a new chance to begin again, to replace old habits with new ones, and to rediscover the calm, confident person you were always meant to be.

ജ്ജ

8

COMMITTING YOURSELF

The Power of Setting Goals

Committing to a positive attitude is not something that happens automatically. It requires deliberate effort and consistency, much like training a muscle. One of the most effective ways to strengthen this commitment is by setting clear, meaningful goals. Many people wonder why they should set goals when they already have one overarching objective: to become more positive. But while developing a positive attitude is indeed the ultimate aim, goals serve as the stepping stones that lead you there. They help you translate broad intentions into daily actions that bring real progress.

Think of your overall goal, building a positive attitude, as a large painting. The painting will only come to life when you add one brushstroke at a time. Each smaller goal is one of those brushstrokes. It might seem insignificant on its own, but together they form the complete picture. Setting small, specific goals helps prevent feelings of overwhelm. Large aspirations can often feel daunting, but when you divide them into manageable parts, you make it easier to take consistent action. Achieving these smaller targets keeps you motivated and provides a sense of accomplishment that fuels your momentum.

Another important reason for setting goals is that they allow you to measure your growth. It is easy to underestimate your own progress when you have no markers to compare it against. You might be putting in tremendous effort, but without tangible milestones, you may not notice how far you have come. Writing down your goals gives structure to your journey. It helps you see where you began, what you have accomplished, and where you need to go next. This clarity brings confidence and direction, both essential ingredients of a positive mindset.

Begin by listing your dreams and turning them into goals. Take a few quiet moments to write down what you truly want from life; what excites you, what feels meaningful, and what aligns with your values. Putting your goals on paper transforms them from fleeting thoughts into concrete intentions. It signals to your mind that these aspirations matter. The simple act of writing them down increases your sense of accountability and commitment. Review your list often, refine it, and keep it somewhere visible to remind yourself of your purpose.

When creating goals, make sure they challenge you. Growth only happens when you step beyond your comfort zone. However, challenges should feel inspiring, not overwhelming. As you write your goals, you might hear that inner voice of doubt whispering things like, "This is too difficult," or "I'll never achieve this." Recognise those thoughts, but don't give them power. Instead, focus on what actions will move you closer to your goal. Break each challenge into smaller, achievable steps, and celebrate every bit of progress. The more you act, the more confident you become. Positivity thrives when it is supported by forward movement.

To stay enthusiastic, approach your goals with curiosity and creativity. If you have tried something before and it didn't work, think about what could be done differently this time. Explore new methods, tools, or learning opportunities that might open fresh possibilities. Sometimes progress requires unlearning habits that no longer serve you. Be flexible and willing to experiment. This not only helps you reach your goals but also keeps your journey interesting and dynamic. Learning new skills or refining existing ones strengthens your sense of control and self-belief.

The process of goal setting also teaches discipline. When you set deadlines and stick to them, you build trust in your own word. Each completed task reinforces the belief that you are capable of following through. Over time, this discipline spills into other areas of your life, creating a strong foundation for long-term positivity. Your confidence grows not just from achieving your goals but from realising that you are in charge of your direction.

Remember that commitment is not about perfection; it is about persistence. Some days you will move quickly, other days more slowly, and that is completely fine. What matters most is that you keep showing up for yourself. Each small step you take adds up. Every action rooted in intention brings you closer to the person you wish to become. When your goals align with your desire for positivity, they stop feeling like obligations and start feeling like growth opportunities.

In the end, the power of goal setting lies in its ability to turn a hopeful attitude into tangible progress. It gives shape to your optimism and transforms it into focused, purposeful action. When you set goals that inspire you, track your progress, and remain flexible in your approach, you will find that positivity is no longer an abstract idea but becomes a lived experience. And with each goal achieved, your confidence and enthusiasm for life will only continue to grow.

ഇര

9

HELP AT HAND

Crafting a Daily Schedule of Positive Activities

Each day brings with it twenty-four hours of opportunity. How you spend that time determines not only what you achieve but also how you feel about yourself and the world around you. Building a positive attitude is not just about what you think; it is also about what you do. By consciously filling your days with meaningful, uplifting activities, you create an environment that nurtures optimism, confidence, and calm. Your daily schedule becomes a reflection of your mindset, and your mindset, in turn, shapes the quality of your life.

Creating a routine filled with positive activities is one of the most practical ways to strengthen your emotional well-being. It gives structure to your day, balances your energy, and ensures that you are not leaving your mood to chance. Begin by asking yourself what activities make you feel genuinely happy and fulfilled. These do not have to be complicated or time-consuming. Sometimes the smallest habits, such as listening to music, spending time outdoors, or connecting with a friend, can make the biggest difference.

Start your day with intention. The first hour of your morning sets the tone for everything that follows. Instead of rushing through it, take a few moments to do something that centres you. This could be as simple as stretching, taking deep breaths, or writing down a few things you are grateful for. A calm and purposeful start signals to your mind that you are in control of the day ahead. Even ten minutes of quiet reflection can ground you and create a sense of direction.

Including physical activity in your schedule is another essential step toward positivity. Movement releases endorphins, which are the body's natural feel-good chemicals, which reduce stress and boost mood. You do not need an elaborate gym routine to benefit from exercise. A brisk walk in the park, a quick dance session in your living room, or a few minutes of yoga can energise both body and mind. Being outdoors amplifies this effect. The natural world has a remarkable ability to restore perspective. A walk surrounded by trees or the sound of birds can calm the mind, refresh your thoughts, and remind you of the simple joys of being alive.

Alongside physical movement, find time each day for something creative. Creativity is an outlet for self-expression, and it helps redirect the mind from worry to imagination. You might enjoy painting, journaling, gardening, cooking, or even learning a new instrument. The point is not perfection but engagement. When you create, you enter a state of flow, a moment where time fades and you are completely immersed in what you are doing. This flow state not only reduces stress but also reinforces confidence and satisfaction.

Music is another simple yet powerful addition to your daily routine. The rhythms and melodies we choose affect our emotions deeply. Upbeat music can lift your spirits and motivate you, while gentle, calming sounds can help you unwind after a long day. Build a few playlists that suit your different moods, one for motivation, one for relaxation, and one simply for joy. Let music accompany your moments of quiet or movement, allowing it to guide your emotional rhythm throughout the day.

Connection is also vital to a balanced, positive routine. Human beings are social creatures, and meaningful interactions play a crucial role in emotional health. Make time to talk to people who uplift and support you. A quick chat, a message of appreciation, or a shared laugh can instantly lighten your mood. Choose relationships that add value to your life, and nurture them through genuine communication and gratitude. Just as positivity grows when shared, so does resilience.

As you plan your day, include moments of rest and reflection. Constant activity without pause can lead to burnout, even when the activities are enjoyable. Schedule small breaks where you can breathe, stretch, or simply pause to notice how you feel. Reflect on what went well and what you are grateful for. These quiet pauses help you stay connected to yourself and prevent stress from accumulating. They remind you that slowing down is not a waste of time but an act of self-care.

It is important that your daily schedule feels flexible and personal. There is no single formula for positivity. What energises one person may not appeal to another. Experiment with different routines until you find a rhythm that feels natural. You might prefer to exercise in the morning, journal in the evening, or spend your weekends exploring creative hobbies. What matters most is that each day contains something that nourishes your spirit and strengthens your sense of well-being.

Consistency is key. The power of positive activities lies in repetition. When you regularly engage in things that bring joy, relaxation, and meaning, your mind begins to expect and seek positivity. Over time, this builds emotional resilience. The more balanced your daily schedule becomes, the more capable you are of handling challenges with patience and grace. A well-rounded day supports a well-rounded mind.

Your life is built one day at a time. By filling each day with moments that inspire, relax, and uplift you, you turn time itself into a tool for transformation. Whether it is through movement, creativity, connection, or reflection, your daily activities can become a living expression of positivity. The more you design your days around joy and purpose, the more naturally positivity becomes a part of who you are.

Here are some ideas for how you can set up a meaningful daily routine:

1. **Begin the Day with Stillness**

   The first minutes after waking determine the tone of your entire day. Before reaching for your phone or checking messages, sit quietly for a few minutes. Breathe deeply, stretch gently, or reflect on a single thought that inspires calm and purpose. This moment of stillness acts as a mental reset. It reminds you that focus is a choice you make, not a mood you wait for.

2. **Set Three Intentional Priorities**

   Each morning, write down the three tasks or goals that matter most. This limits decision fatigue and gives your mind a clear direction. When everything seems urgent, nothing truly gets your attention. By identifying your top priorities, you conserve energy and guide your concentration toward meaningful outcomes instead of distractions.

3. **Schedule Pauses for Renewal**

   Focus is not endurance alone; it is rhythm. Between work or study sessions, take short breaks to stretch, breathe, or step outside. Walk without your phone, look at something natural, or rest your eyes in silence. These brief intervals of restoration prevent burnout and make returning to work easier and more effective.

4. **Guard Your Digital Boundaries**

   Design your routine so your devices serve your goals, not control them. Avoid screens for the first and last hour of the day. Keep your workspace free of unnecessary tabs or alerts. Replace random scrolling with intentional reading or listening. A quiet digital environment gives your mind room to breathe and think.

5. **Anchor Each Day with Meaning**

   Concentration thrives when the mind feels connected to purpose. Include one small act each day that nourishes the spirit: reading something uplifting, spending time in nature, or expressing gratitude. These acts restore balance and remind you that attention is not just a skill, but a way of living with awareness.

ഇ൬

10

REDISCOVERING THE CHILD WITHIN

Embracing Wonder and Dreams

There is a big difference between being *childish* and being *childlike*. The first comes from immaturity, but the second springs from innocence, curiosity, and joy. Somewhere along the journey from childhood to adulthood, many of us lose touch with that natural sense of wonder that once defined us. We become busy, serious, and cautious. The child who once laughed easily and dreamed fearlessly begins to fade under layers of responsibility, expectation, and fear of failure. Rediscovering that child within is one of the most powerful ways to reignite positivity in your life.

Think back for a moment to your early years. What made you happy then? Was it the smell of rain, the sound of laughter, or the excitement of learning something new? As children, we were quick to forgive, eager to explore, and endlessly curious. We didn't dwell on the past or overthink the future. Every day felt like a new adventure.

That natural openness allowed us to experience joy in its purest form. But as we grow older, we start carrying emotional baggage; disappointments, grudges, and doubts, that weigh us down. We trade curiosity for certainty, spontaneity for caution, and playfulness for control. Over time, this distance from our inner child dulls our enthusiasm and narrows our perspective.

To build a truly positive mindset, it is essential to reconnect with that part of yourself that still believes in possibilities. This doesn't mean ignoring responsibilities or being unrealistic. It means bringing back the same openness, imagination, and trust that once came so easily. The child within you has not disappeared; it has only been quieted by years of worry and self-criticism. You can awaken it again by allowing yourself to be present, curious, and unafraid to dream.

One of the simplest ways to rediscover your inner child is to start afresh every day. Children rarely hold on to anger or disappointment for long. If a friend hurts them, they might cry, but soon enough, they laugh together again. Adults, on the other hand, tend to carry emotional residue from one day to the next. We replay old conversations, revisit mistakes, and drag yesterday's worries into today. To be childlike is to let go of what no longer serves you. Each morning, remind yourself that today is a clean slate. The past cannot be changed, but the present moment is yours to shape. When you learn to see each day as a new beginning, life starts to feel lighter and full of promise again.

Another way to nurture the child within is by rekindling your sense of wonder. Children have an extraordinary ability to find magic in the ordinary. They can spend hours watching clouds move, marvel at a butterfly, or laugh at something simple. Somewhere along the way, adults begin to overlook these small joys. We rush through life so focused on what's next that we forget to notice what is now. Take a few minutes each day to look around you with fresh eyes. Watch the sunrise or sunset, listen to the sound of birds, or notice the texture of leaves swaying in the wind. These moments remind you that beauty still exists everywhere. It only asks to be noticed. Wonder renews your spirit and makes you more grateful for life itself.

Then comes the most powerful trait of all: the ability to dream. As children, we dreamt freely and without limits. We wanted to fly, to build, to create, to change the world. We didn't question whether it was possible. But as adults, we learn to doubt. We tell ourselves that dreams are impractical or that we've missed our chance. Rediscovering your childlike nature means daring to dream again. It means permitting yourself to imagine the best possible version of your life. Dreaming does not mean ignoring reality; it means expanding it. Every great achievement began as someone's dream. Allow yourself to believe, once more, that you have what it takes to make your dreams real.

To reconnect with this part of yourself, try engaging in activities that once brought you joy as a child. Draw, dance, play, or build something with your hands. These simple acts open your creative energy and reconnect you to feelings of freedom and possibility. They remind you that joy does not have to be earned, it can be created, anytime, by choosing to live fully in the moment.

Being childlike also means trusting others more openly and forgiving more easily. Children assume the best in people until given a reason not to. As adults, we tend to do the opposite, often expecting disappointment or rejection. Try softening your approach. Give people the benefit of the doubt. Let kindness guide your interactions. This openness does not make you naïve; it makes you human. Trust and compassion are not weaknesses, they are strengths that build resilience and connection.

Most importantly, remember that positivity is not about pretending life is perfect. It is about keeping your spirit alive even when things are difficult. The child within you knows how to recover from setbacks because it naturally believes that joy will return. When you begin to see life through that lens again, challenges become lessons, and even small moments become sources of happiness.

Reclaiming your inner child is like finding a long-lost friend, one who knows how to laugh, forgive, and dream without limits. By reconnecting with that part of yourself, you invite playfulness, curiosity, and creativity back into your life. These qualities are the true foundation of a positive attitude. They remind you that no matter how serious life becomes, you can always approach it with lightness, wonder, and hope. The child within you is still waiting to be heard. When you start listening, joy begins to speak again.

ജ്യ

L E A P Learning Empowerment & Achieving Potential

Amplifying Your Inner Voice: Communication With Yourself

11

KNOWING AND USING YOUR STRENGTHS

Your Pillars of Power

Everyone has strengths, but surprisingly few people recognise them. Often, what comes easily to us feels ordinary. We assume, "If I can do it without trying too hard, it must not be that special." In reality, those effortless qualities are the very things that make you unique. Your natural abilities, perspectives, and patterns of excellence form the foundation for confidence, motivation, and achievement.

A positive attitude doesn't begin with ignoring weaknesses. It begins with honouring your strengths. When you understand what energises you and where you naturally perform best, you stop swimming against the current. You align effort with ability, and life begins to feel more balanced, productive, and fulfilling. Working from your strengths does not mean you refuse to grow; it means you build from a stable core rather than from insecurity.

Recognising strengths can also improve how you relate to others. People who understand their capabilities communicate more clearly, delegate more wisely, and support others without fear of competition. They no longer feel threatened by someone else's success because they know their own lane and contribution. Strength awareness, then, becomes the bridge between confidence and cooperation.

Introspect on Strengths

To discover your strengths, start with quiet reflection. Step away from distractions, find stillness, and ask yourself a few essential questions: *What am I doing when I feel most alive? When do I lose track of time because I'm so engaged? Which tasks leave me feeling fulfilled rather than drained?*

Your answers to these questions often reveal patterns that point to your genuine abilities. Strengths are not always dramatic or showy; sometimes they are subtle, like patience, empathy, consistency, or creative thinking. These traits may not attract immediate recognition, but they hold immense power in shaping your personal and professional relationships.

It's also helpful to look outward for perspective. Ask five people you trust to describe one quality they value in you. Their answers may surprise you and broaden your understanding of how your strengths show up in real life. Sometimes, the reflection others hold up becomes the mirror that finally helps you see yourself clearly.

As you gather these insights, write them down. Treat this as a living document that you can revisit and refine. Your strengths evolve, shaped by new experiences and challenges. Recognising them is not a one-time exercise but a continuous process of learning who you are and how you operate at your best.

Verbalise It

Once you identify your strengths, begin to voice them. Speaking affirmatively about your abilities is not arrogance, but clarity. It trains your subconscious to believe in your potential and prepares you to act from confidence rather than hesitation.

Every time you say, "I am good at solving problems," or "I am a compassionate listener," you strengthen that belief internally. Over time, it becomes part of your identity. When your language aligns with your capability, your energy, communication, and results follow suit. You approach challenges with steadier composure because you have rehearsed belief instead of doubt.

This is also how positive self-talk connects to performance. Athletes, leaders, and artists use verbal affirmations as mental conditioning tools. The brain responds to repeated language cues, creating new neural pathways that support behaviour change. The more you affirm your strengths, the more naturally your actions reflect them.

Go With It

Once you recognise and affirm your strengths, it is time to use them. Strengths are meant to be expressed, not stored away. Build your personal and professional goals around them, and you'll find that progress comes with greater ease and enjoyment. When you design your life in alignment with your strengths, challenges become opportunities to apply what you already know works for you.

At the same time, don't try to be good at everything. Nobody can. Focus on refining what you do best and partner with people who fill in the gaps. Collaboration is the most practical form of humility—it acknowledges that everyone brings something different to the table. Together, your collective strengths can accomplish far more than individual effort ever could.

Finally, remember that your strengths are living resources. They are not fixed; they grow as you grow. The more you nurture them through learning, feedback, and practice, the stronger they become. Just as a seed draws sunlight and nutrients to flourish, your inner strengths attract the people, opportunities, and resources you need when you act from authenticity. Every strength you embrace expands your capacity to lead a positive, purposeful, and fulfilling life.

༻༺

13

SUBLIMINAL LEARNING

Reinforcing Positivity from Within

Starting your day with positive thoughts sets the tone for everything that follows. The way you begin your morning, what you listen to, what you say to yourself, and how you feel, can shape your attitude for the entire day. A few encouraging words or uplifting sounds can act like mental vitamins, strengthening your emotional balance and keeping negativity at bay. When you consistently focus on the good, you start to notice more of it, and that awareness begins to transform how you think, feel, and act.

But maintaining positivity isn't always about conscious effort or constant motivation. Sometimes, your mind can learn quietly in the background. This is where subliminal learning comes in. It is one of the most fascinating and effective tools for personal growth because it taps into the subconscious, the part of your mind that shapes habits, emotions, and automatic responses.

Understanding Subliminal Learning

Subliminal learning happens when information reaches your subconscious without your active focus. It bypasses the critical, filtering part of your conscious mind and speaks directly to the deeper layers of thought that influence behaviour. In simple terms, it's like feeding your mind positive nourishment without even noticing it.

Imagine listening to a calm voice saying things like, "You are capable," "You are calm," or "You attract success." These messages might play softly in the background while you read, relax, work, or even sleep. Your conscious mind may not catch every word, but your subconscious does. Over time, these affirmations settle into your thought patterns, quietly shaping how you perceive yourself and your potential.

This technique has been used in many forms; from motivational recordings and relaxation tracks to background music with embedded affirmations. The purpose is simple: to replace old, limiting beliefs with new, empowering ones. By repeatedly hearing positive messages, your brain begins to adopt them as truth, and your attitude naturally starts to align with those beliefs.

How Subliminal Learning Works

Your subconscious mind is always active, even when you are not paying attention. It absorbs sounds, emotions, and messages from your environment. When you expose yourself to positive cues repeatedly, these begin to form mental associations. Eventually, your mind starts responding as if those positive messages are facts, influencing how you think and behave automatically.

For example, if you often tell yourself, "I'm not good enough," your brain wires that thought into your mental structure. Subliminal learning flips this pattern by reinforcing the opposite message: "I am capable and deserving." Over time, this new belief becomes your default response. The result is a quieter mind, greater self-confidence, and a natural sense of optimism that doesn't need to be forced.

Incorporating Subliminal Learning into Daily Life

There are many ways to integrate subliminal learning into your routine. You can listen to guided audios that contain affirmations related to confidence, peace, or success while you work, rest, or commute. Some people play these softly at night while sleeping, allowing the subconscious to process them without distraction.

You can also combine subliminal learning with visualisation. As you listen to affirmations, picture yourself embodying them: see yourself succeeding, smiling, or speaking with confidence. This mental imagery strengthens the connection between thought and feeling, helping your mind adopt positivity as its natural state.

However, it is important to remember that subliminal learning complements active self-improvement. It does not replace conscious action, reflection, or personal responsibility. It reinforces what you are already working toward. Think of it as the quiet background music to your growth; a supportive rhythm that keeps you tuned to positivity even when life feels challenging.

Building the Habit

To get the most from subliminal learning, consistency is key. Use short, clear affirmations and listen regularly for at least a few minutes each day. Choose messages that feel authentic to you. Generic or unrealistic statements can sometimes create resistance in the mind, so tailor them to your goals. For example, instead of "I am always perfect," try "I am learning and improving every day." The more believable the message, the more easily your subconscious accepts it.

Remember that your mind responds to repetition and emotion. When you listen with intention, even if passively, your subconscious begins to align with what you desire. Over time, you will notice subtle but real changes: improved mood, reduced anxiety, more constructive reactions, and a stronger sense of calm confidence.

ꝏ

14

PREPARATORY RELAXATION EXERCISES FOR PRODUCTIVE SELF-TALK

Before you begin your self-talk practice, one essential step can make all the difference: learning how to relax. A calm body and mind create the right environment for positive suggestions to take root. When you are relaxed, your thoughts slow down, your breathing evens out, and your subconscious becomes more receptive to new ideas. Self-talk works best when it flows into a quiet, focused mind rather than competing with tension, distraction, or fatigue.

Relaxation, therefore, is not a luxury before self-talk but the foundation. Think of it as clearing a field before planting new seeds. The more prepared and open your mind is, the more effectively it absorbs and reinforces the messages you give it.

Finding the Right Space

Start by creating your personal relaxation space, your calm zone. Choose a quiet, comfortable corner where you can be alone for a few minutes without interruption. It doesn't have to be fancy; it only needs to feel peaceful. You might pick a spot near a window, a cosy chair, or a small corner of your bedroom. If noise is an issue, earplugs or soft instrumental music can help create an atmosphere of calm.

Timing matters too. Avoid rushing into self-talk when you are exhausted, distracted, or anxious. Instead, find a time when your energy feels settled, perhaps early in the morning or before bed. Even ten uninterrupted minutes can make a big difference. When you consciously carve out time and space for yourself, you send a quiet signal to your mind that this practice matters

Settling into Comfort

Once you are in your chosen spot, take a moment to get comfortable. Lie flat on your back or sit upright with your spine supported. Your arms can rest loosely by your sides, palms facing upward. Keep your body relaxed but alert.

Begin by closing your eyes and taking a few deep, slow breaths. Inhale through your nose, hold for a brief moment, and exhale gently through your mouth. Feel your shoulders drop and your muscles soften with each breath. There is no need to force anything. Just allow your body to find its own rhythm of ease.

As you settle in, start your internal dialogue with kindness. Speak softly to yourself using positive and realistic statements such as:

"It's okay if I take time to learn this technique."

"I am patient with myself as I grow more comfortable with self-talk."

"My mind and body are working together to create calm and focus."

You are not just saying words; you are setting an emotional tone, one of patience, safety, and self-compassion. Over time, this attitude of gentle encouragement builds trust within yourself and deepens the effectiveness of your self-talk practice.

The Role of Comfort and Privacy

Comfort is essential because it helps your body release tension, and privacy helps your mind feel safe. When you know that no one is watching or listening, you can speak openly and without self-consciousness. You might even find that your self-talk naturally becomes more honest and authentic in a private setting.

Before you begin, handle small physical distractions; adjust the room temperature, wear loose clothing, drink some water, and take care of basic needs so your mind can focus fully. If you have family or roommates, let them know you need some quiet time. Small preparations like these make a big difference in your mental readiness.

Think of your self-talk session as a personal meeting with yourself. You are both the listener and the speaker, the mentor and the student. You deserve this space and time to focus on your inner well-being.

Building a Consistent Routine

Like any meaningful habit, relaxation before self-talk becomes more effective with consistency. The goal is not perfection, but rhythm. Over time, your body learns to associate your chosen spot, posture, and breathing with a sense of calm focus. Even on stressful days, returning to that same practice will help you transition more easily into a peaceful state.

In the beginning, your mind may wander, or you might feel restless. That's normal. Instead of getting frustrated, use gentle curiosity. Notice your thoughts, then return your attention to your breathing or to a soothing word like "peace," "focus," or "calm." The more often you do this, the easier it becomes to enter that quiet, receptive space.

Ultimately, the purpose of these relaxation exercises is not to escape reality, but to prepare yourself for a deeper connection with your thoughts, with your goals, and with your best self.

ꟷ

15

USING EVERYDAY PHRASES IN YOUR SELF-TALK SESSION

Once you have created a calm space and learned how to relax your body and mind, you are ready to begin your self-talk practice. Sometimes, you might start your session with a clear goal, perhaps building confidence before a big presentation or overcoming a specific fear. But on other days, your aim might be broader: to strengthen your mindset, improve focus, or simply feel more balanced and positive.

Self-talk is flexible. It adapts to your needs, your mood, and your moment. You don't always need a grand purpose to begin. What matters most is that you speak to yourself with honesty, intention, and care. Over time, these quiet conversations will become a powerful force shaping how you think, feel, and act.

The Power of Everyday Language

The words you use every day have an immense influence on your emotional state. They form the soundtrack of your inner world. Positive self-talk replaces the harsh or doubtful phrases that often run unnoticed in the background with words that build trust and encouragement. By repeating affirming statements regularly, you create new mental habits that support growth and resilience.

Simple, grounded phrases are often more effective than grand or overly ambitious ones. They work because they sound real, like something a wise, encouraging friend might say to you. When your affirmations feel believable, your subconscious mind accepts them more easily, and your self-talk becomes natural rather than forced.

Below are examples of affirmations you can use in different areas of your life. Feel free to adapt them to suit your voice and goals.

For Focus and Progress

"Every time I practise, I improve."

"I focus on what matters and make steady progress."

"Small, consistent actions lead to big results."

"I stay calm and centred even when challenges arise."

"I give my best to every task, one step at a time."

For Confidence and Self-Belief

"I trust my abilities and act with confidence."

"I am capable of handling whatever comes my way."

"I speak clearly, think clearly, and move forward with purpose."

"I am learning to believe in myself fully."

"I deserve to take up space and be heard."

For Balance and Peace

"I create harmony between work, rest, and play."

"I give time to my loved ones and to myself."

"Peace begins in my mind and flows into everything I do."

"I allow myself moments of rest without guilt."

"I find calm even in busy days."

For Resilience and Growth

"Setbacks are lessons, not failures."

"I recover quickly and learn from every experience."

"I choose patience over frustration."

"I can adapt, adjust, and rise again."

"Every challenge strengthens me."

For Self-Worth and Gratitude

"I am enough just as I am, even as I grow."

"I recognise my effort and celebrate my progress."

"I am grateful for all that I have and all that I am becoming."

"I treat myself with the same kindness I offer others."

"I honour my values every single day."

For Relationships and Connection

"I communicate with honesty and empathy."

"I attract positive, supportive people into my life."

"I forgive easily and release resentment."

"I am open to giving and receiving love freely."

"I bring calm, understanding, and kindness into my interactions."

For Acceptance and Letting Go

"I focus on what I can control and let go of what I cannot."

"I accept the past and move forward with peace."

"I make peace with imperfection and learn from it."

"I choose to see endings as new beginnings."

"I am learning to trust life's timing."

These affirmations are starting points. Use them as they are, or rewrite them in your own words. The key is to make them sound like *you*, believable, gentle, and encouraging. Speak them aloud, write them in a journal, or play them in your mind during quiet moments. The more familiar they become, the more they will shape your thoughts, emotions, and behaviour.

Personalising Your Self-Talk

To make your self-talk truly powerful, tailor it to your goals and values. Begin by writing down what you want to improve: confidence, patience, health, or happiness, and then create simple statements that reflect those intentions. For instance:

Instead of "I want to stop being nervous," say, "I am learning to stay calm and focused."

Instead of "I will try to be more positive," say, "I choose to see the good in every situation."

This small shift from desire to declaration helps your mind focus on progress rather than lack. It teaches your subconscious to act as if the improvement is already underway, reinforcing that belief through action.

Making It a Habit

Use these phrases daily, while relaxing, walking, journaling, or before bed. Speak them out loud when you can; your voice adds conviction and energy to your thoughts. Consistency matters more than intensity. Repetition turns words into beliefs and beliefs into behaviour.

You may not notice changes immediately, but gradually, your tone will soften, your self-trust will grow, and your reactions to challenges will become calmer. Over time, these small moments of conscious speech will transform your inner world, and by extension, your outer one.

Remember, self-talk is not about pretending everything is perfect. It's about creating a language of support that helps you stay grounded and hopeful, even when life feels uncertain. Your words can become your greatest ally—steady, kind, and quietly powerful.

16

USING POSITIVE SELF-TALK TO IMPROVE YOUR PERSONALITY

Some people might ask, "Why would I want to use positive self-talk to improve my personality? I like who I am." If that's true for you, if you are comfortable in your own skin and happy with the person you are, then you have already mastered one of life's rarest achievements. Authentic self-acceptance naturally radiates confidence and warmth. People who feel good about themselves rarely need to force charm or seek approval; their comfort becomes their charisma.

But not everyone feels that way. Many people struggle with self-doubt, shyness, or insecurity. They may want to connect with others yet hold back out of fear of judgment or rejection. The irony is that this very hesitation often gets misread. What feels like nervousness on the inside can appear as aloofness or disinterest on the outside. Over time, this misunderstanding forms a cycle, others misinterpret your quietness, you withdraw further, and the distance between how you feel and how you are perceived grows wider.

Positive self-talk can break that cycle. It helps you re-align how you *see yourself* with how you *want to be seen*. The goal isn't to change your personality, it's to express your best qualities more confidently and consistently.

How Positive Self-Talk Shapes Perception

Your personality is the outward expression of your inner thoughts and beliefs. When your self-talk is filled with doubt ("I'm not interesting," "I'm too quiet," "I always say the wrong thing"), your body language reflects it; tense posture, minimal eye contact, hesitant speech. But when your inner dialogue shifts to support you ("I'm easy to talk to," "I bring calm to conversations," "People enjoy my company"), your energy changes. You relax. You smile more naturally. You engage more openly.

Positive self-talk doesn't magically alter your personality traits, but it changes how you *feel about yourself*. And that change influences how others experience you. When you see yourself as approachable, kind, or confident, your actions unconsciously reinforce those traits. Gradually, others begin to mirror that perception, turning self-belief into social ease.

This is similar to how a sincere compliment from a friend can brighten your day. It doesn't change who you are, but it reminds you of what's already good and worth showing more often. Self-talk is like giving yourself that compliment every day until it becomes part of how you live.

Practical Steps to Improve Your Personality Through Self-Talk

1. **Reflect on Your Self-Perception**
   Begin by listing what you've said to yourself about your personality, both positive and negative. Include compliments you've received

as well as criticisms you've absorbed over time. This exercise helps you recognise the stories you've been repeating internally, many of which might not even be true. Awareness is the first step toward change.

2. **Repeat Genuine Compliments**

   When others compliment you, don't dismiss it or deflect it. Write it down. Read it aloud later as part of your self-talk. Repetition helps you internalise those affirmations until you no longer need external validation. For example:

   "I'm a good listener."

   "People feel comfortable around me."

   "I bring a sense of calm and positivity to my environment."

   These reminders help reinforce traits that others already see in you.

3. **Create Your Own Positive Declarations**

   Now, write a list of qualities you would like to strengthen or express more often, traits like patience, warmth, confidence, curiosity, or humour. Then craft affirmations around them. For instance:

   "I speak clearly and confidently."

   "I enjoy meeting new people and learning their stories."

   "My presence makes people feel at ease."

   "I am open, kind, and approachable."

   "I trust myself to handle any social situation with grace."

   Say them regularly, ideally aloud. Over time, your tone, expressions, and posture will start to align with these messages.

4. **Focus Beyond Appearance**

   While it's natural to want to feel good about how you look, remember that physical appearance changes with time. Personality, the way you make people feel, lasts. You can acknowledge your physical features ("I carry myself well," "I like my smile") but let your affirmations emphasise traits that reflect your essence: your empathy, humour, creativity, or reliability.

5. **Reinforce and Reflect**

   Each week, take a few minutes to note how your self-talk has influenced your interactions. Did you smile more easily? Speak up in a meeting? Start a conversation you might've avoided? These small observations build awareness and prove that change is taking root.

   As you reinforce your values and appreciate your growth, you'll notice subtle but powerful shifts, more confidence in your voice, ease in your body language, and openness in your relationships. The more you affirm your worth, the more others will reflect it to you.

Turning the Cycle Around

Positive self-talk reverses the old pattern of self-doubt and misunderstanding. Where there was hesitation, there is now presence. Where there was defensiveness, there is calm. Each affirmation becomes a brick in a new foundation—one built on authenticity and confidence instead of anxiety and fear.

In time, your personality will not feel like something you have to "improve." It will feel like something you are finally *allowing* to shine.

ഌ

L E A P Learning Empowerment & Achieving Potential

Living the Transformation: Confidence, Health, and Momentum

17

THE RIPPLE EFFECT

Becoming a More Confident You

There's a witty quote by Herm Albright that says, "A positive attitude may not solve all your problems, but it will annoy enough people to make it worth the effort." While we don't aim to annoy anyone, the truth behind the humour is powerful . Attitude is not just a personal outlook; it shapes how others experience you. Winston Churchill captured it perfectly when he said, "Attitude is a little thing that makes a big difference." The same is true for confidence. It begins within you, but its effects ripple far beyond.

Confidence is not something people are born with. It is built, one experience at a time, through learning, repetition, and reflection. Think of it as the bridge between belief and action. You may know what to do and even want to do it, but confidence is what allows you to take that first step. It transforms a thought into movement. Every time you try something new, succeed a little, or simply face discomfort without giving up, you strengthen the foundation of your self-trust. Over time, that quiet self-trust becomes confidence.

Most people think confidence comes from achieving big things, but in truth, it grows from small, steady moments of courage. Every act of following through on your intentions, such as finishing a project, keeping a promise, speaking up in a meeting, teaches your mind to trust itself. That is how confidence compounds: small victories build self-assurance, and that self-assurance fuels larger victories. This loop of belief and action is what psychologists call reinforcement, and it is one of the most powerful tools for emotional growth.

But confidence is not only about how you feel inside; it's also about how you connect with others. A confident person communicates differently. They are more present, more grounded, and more attuned. They don't need to dominate a conversation or prove their worth. Instead, their confidence shows through calmness, clarity, and empathy. They listen fully, speak with intention, and bring a sense of stability to the space around them. Confidence is not about being louder than others; it's about being sure of your voice and generous with your attention.

When you start to feel confident, you also begin to influence others more naturally. People are drawn to those who radiate calm assurance. This is the true ripple effect of confidence, your energy becomes contagious. Your steady attitude can diffuse tension, inspire motivation, and help others believe in their own ability to handle life's challenges. You begin to lead not by authority, but by example. A positive, confident person makes others feel safe enough to rise, too.

To build this kind of confidence, awareness is key. Pay attention to the stories you tell yourself throughout the day. Everyone has an inner voice that comments, judges, worries, and reassures. Often, that voice is harsher than it needs to be. When you become conscious of it, you can begin to redirect it toward constructive, encouraging dialogue. Replace "I can't handle this" with "I'm learning to manage this." Swap "I always mess things up" with "I've handled tough things before; I can figure this out too." The more often you guide your thoughts this way, the faster your brain learns a new habit of optimism.

True confidence is not about pretending to have all the answers. It's about trusting yourself enough to keep learning. This mindset transforms fear into curiosity. Instead of avoiding challenges, you begin to explore them. You take courses, ask questions, and improve skills not to fix your flaws, but to expand your capabilities. When you meet life this way, with openness rather than defensiveness, you naturally become more confident because you no longer fear the unknown.

The most confident people are not the ones who never make mistakes. They are the ones who have learned to recover gracefully. They understand that failure is not a verdict; it's information. A setback is not the end of confidence but the start of resilience. Each time you rise after a fall, your belief in yourself deepens. Confidence built this way is not fragile. It doesn't depend on success or applause; it stands on the quiet strength of experience.

And with that strength comes another kind of maturity, humility. Real confidence does not shout or compete. It listens, learns, and uplifts. It allows you to take feedback without feeling attacked and to acknowledge others' strengths without feeling diminished. Humility keeps confidence from turning into ego, grounding it in empathy and awareness. When you reach this stage, confidence becomes less about proving yourself and more about contributing to the world around you.

That is the essence of the ripple effect. Your confidence begins within you, but it never stays there. It spreads through how you speak, how you behave, and how you inspire. The calm, steady energy of a self-assured person brings out the best in others, it permits them to believe in themselves, too. A confident person doesn't just change their own life; they influence the emotional climate of every room they enter.

The more you live with this mindset, the more you'll notice how it affects everything: your performance at work, your relationships, your health, even your creativity. Confidence becomes a kind of quiet power, not showy, not loud, but deeply stabilising. It reminds you that you don't have to wait for permission to grow. You are already enough to begin.

18

A HEALTHY MIND, A HEALTHY BODY

The Vital Connection

Science has long confirmed what ancient wisdom always knew: the mind and body are deeply connected. Every thought, every emotion, and every belief you hold sends ripples through your entire system, influencing how you feel both physically and mentally. You are not a collection of separate parts; you are one complete, self-managing being. Your thoughts, hormones, immune system, and emotions work together in a constant, delicate conversation.

Modern biomedical research has shown a clear link between optimism and health. People with positive attitudes tend to have stronger immune systems, better cardiovascular health, and lower levels of inflammation. In contrast, those burdened by chronic negativity or stress experience hormonal imbalances, sleep disruption, and an increased risk of disease. Your thoughts don't just stay in your mind; they shape your biology in measurable ways.

Stress is one of the clearest examples of this connection. When your mind perceives threat or pressure, your body releases cortisol and adrenaline. These hormones are useful in short bursts because they sharpen focus and fuel quick responses. But when stress becomes constant, these same hormones start to damage the body. They suppress immunity, elevate blood pressure, and drain mental reserves. A consistently negative mindset keeps the body in this "fight or flight" mode, exhausting its ability to heal, recover, and thrive.

The reverse is also true. When you think positively, your brain releases dopamine, serotonin, and endorphins, which are natural mood lifters that strengthen your immune system and energise your cells. Positivity is not naive thinking; it is biochemical empowerment. It helps your body move from a state of survival to one of balance and growth. People who maintain a hopeful, forward-looking outlook are not only happier but also physically stronger and more resilient.

This mind-body connection becomes even more important as we age. Research shows that people with an optimistic attitude tend to live longer, sometimes by as much as seven years. Their bodies age more gracefully because their minds stay engaged, curious, and proactive. A positive mindset toward ageing allows people to adapt and enjoy life's later stages with energy and gratitude.

However, understanding the science is only the first step. The real challenge is applying it consistently. Many of us know that positive thinking improves well-being, yet we struggle to maintain it when life becomes overwhelming. That is why it is so important to slow down, simplify, and make space for recovery. Sleep well, breathe deeply, move regularly, and spend time doing what nourishes your spirit.

These are not luxuries; they are foundations of health. When you allow yourself rest and joy, you help your body repair itself and keep your mind clear.

Positive affirmations can also support this process. When you speak kindly to yourself, your body listens. Each affirmation sends a signal of safety and balance to your nervous system. Over time, this gentle reinforcement can change how your body responds to stress. Phrases like "I am calm and capable" or "I trust my body to heal" may seem simple, but they train your mind to send healing messages instead of anxious ones.

Thoughts, however, must be paired with action. Positive thinking without healthy living is incomplete. To experience the true benefits of the mind-body connection, your habits must align with your mindset. Eat nourishing food, stay active, and build routines that energise rather than deplete you. For example, if you want to get fitter or lose weight, focus not on restriction but on how good movement makes you feel. Visualise how light, strong, and alive you will be. Let that image motivate your choices.

Ultimately, the healthiest people are not those who never get sick but those whose minds and bodies work in harmony. They rest when needed, act with purpose, and handle stress with perspective. They understand that well-being is not about control but about connection, between thought and action, between discipline and ease, between the mind that leads and the body that follows. When both work together, life feels more energetic, more focused, and more whole.

ഗ്ദ

19

SUSTAINING THE SPARK

Living with Purpose and Positive Momentum

By now, you have learned that positivity is not a fleeting emotion or a motivational burst. It is a mindset, a rhythm, a way of living that seeps into everything you do. The real question, then, is not how to become positive, but how to stay that way, how to sustain the spark once it's been lit.

Lasting transformation doesn't come from one grand decision. It grows quietly through small, consistent choices. Each time you speak kindly to yourself, pause before reacting, or choose patience over frustration, you strengthen the foundation of a positive life. These moments may seem minor, but together they create momentum. Over time, positivity stops feeling like an effort and becomes the natural expression of who you are. The goal isn't to stay cheerful at all times but to stay centred, grounded, and capable of returning to balance when life feels uncertain.

There will be days when your energy dips, when old doubts resurface, and when optimism feels like hard work. That's when practice becomes powerful. Instead of fighting those moments, acknowledge them. Pause, breathe, and remind yourself that every lapse is temporary. Return to your affirmations, reflect on your progress, or revisit the goals that once inspired you. Positivity isn't about ignoring challenges, it's about facing them with perspective. Each time you return to your centre, you grow stronger, steadier, and more confident in your ability to navigate change.

As you become more balanced within yourself, you naturally begin to affect others. The calm, assurance, and warmth you cultivate ripple outward. You start noticing how your presence influences those around you; how encouragement can inspire a friend, how patience can ease tension, how kindness can shift the tone of an entire day. The energy you share multiplies and circles back. Helping others is not only an act of compassion; it is a way to renew your own positivity. When you lift someone else, you lift yourself.

Living this way means aligning what you think, say, and do. It means showing up as the same person privately and publicly, in easy times and in challenging ones. This kind of integrity builds deep inner peace because there is no contradiction within you. You act from clarity rather than confusion, purpose rather than impulse. When your choices match your values, life begins to flow with less resistance. You don't have to force positivity. It emerges naturally from a sense of inner alignment.

Growth, however, is not linear. You will have moments of doubt, frustration, or exhaustion. That's part of the process. Think of your journey as a circle rather than a straight path, a cycle of effort, reflection, renewal, and rest. Each phase has its value. When you move through that circle with awareness, every return to mindfulness deepens your stability. The setbacks stop feeling like failures and start feeling like reminders of how far you've come.

Over time, this becomes your lifestyle, a quiet, steady rhythm of living with purpose, authenticity, and compassion. You learn that positivity doesn't mean perfection; it means harmony. It means creating a balance between self-care and contribution, between ambition and rest, between personal peace and social responsibility. You begin to measure success not by how much you achieve, but by how meaningfully you live and how deeply you connect.

The spark that began as self-improvement becomes something larger, a light you carry into the world. You find yourself encouraging others, sharing what helped you, or simply becoming the kind of presence that makes others feel safe and understood. And as you give that energy away, it replenishes you. Positivity, when lived fully, is a cycle of giving and receiving, of growing and grounding. It never truly ends; it renews itself each time you choose awareness over autopilot, gratitude over complaint, and growth over fear.

This is the essence of living with purpose and positive momentum: not the absence of struggle, but the presence of strength; not the pursuit of perfection, but the cultivation of peace. When you live with awareness, gratitude, and compassion, you carry the power to transform both your life and the lives you touch. The light you nurture within yourself becomes a quiet force that moves outward, shaping a kinder, more balanced world.

ℵ

CONCLUSION

Harnessing the Power of Positive Thinking for Lasting Change

Throughout this book, we have explored how attitude, focus, self-talk, and perspective shape the life you live. Every chapter has been a step toward understanding one powerful truth: your mind and your attitude are the architects of your reality. The thoughts you choose, the emotions you nurture, and the beliefs you hold all create the foundation upon which your life is built. When you shift your thinking, your world begins to shift with it.

A positive attitude is not simply about being cheerful. It is about developing a deep sense of control and purpose. It means understanding that while you cannot always choose what happens to you, you can always choose how you respond. By taking charge of your inner world, you begin to influence your outer one. That is how real change begins.

Creating lasting positivity requires awareness and daily practice. Take time each day to connect with yourself, even if it is just for a few minutes. Reflect quietly on the things you are grateful for. Acknowledge the progress you have made and the lessons you have learned.

Gratitude grounds you in the present moment and reminds you that life, even in its imperfections, is full of gifts. This quiet reflection is not a luxury but a necessity. It is how you reset your energy, find balance, and keep perspective amid the noise of everyday life.

Learn to observe your thoughts as they arise. Many of the ideas that fill our minds are habits, patterns formed by years of influence, repetition, and emotion. The good news is that these patterns can be changed. When a negative thought appears, recognise it, and then choose a better one. It may not feel natural at first, but with practice, the mind learns to seek the positive more easily. Over time, optimism becomes a quiet strength that guides your decisions and your relationships.

Visualisation is another simple but powerful way to direct your energy. Picture yourself achieving your goals, living with confidence, and handling challenges calmly. The mind responds to these images as if they were real, building the focus and determination you need to make them come true. This is not wishful thinking. It is training your brain to recognise and act upon opportunities that align with your vision.

Gratitude and visualisation work best when they are combined with action. True positivity is not passive; it is active and engaged. It means choosing words, habits, and relationships that strengthen your mental and physical well-being. It means exercising, resting, and eating well, not because you must, but because your body and mind deserve care. When your thoughts and actions support each other, you begin to live with greater harmony and less resistance.

Equally important is self-belief. Believe deeply in your own potential. Be your own ally. Support yourself the way you would support someone you love. Positive self-talk is not about ignoring your flaws but about recognising your strengths and your capacity to grow. Speak to yourself kindly, with the understanding that every effort you make counts. Celebrate your small victories, because those are the steps that lead to transformation.

As you practice these principles, you will begin to notice how your positivity influences others. When you live with calm and confidence, people around you feel it too. Your energy can inspire change in your family, your workplace, and your community. This is how positivity spreads, quietly but powerfully, through kindness, patience, and the example you set each day.

The connection between your mind, body, and emotions is stronger than most realise. Science continues to show that optimism supports better health, stronger immunity, and longer life. A healthy mind contributes to a healthy body, and both are sustained by a balanced, grateful spirit. When you care for your mental and emotional well-being, your physical vitality follows naturally.

Remember that being positive does not mean being perfect. It means choosing hope when things feel uncertain. It means learning from failure without letting it define you. It means returning, again and again, to that inner place of peace, no matter how many times life tests you. Every challenge you face can strengthen your awareness, deepen your compassion, and refine your purpose.

You now have a set of tools; self-awareness, gratitude, positive self-talk, affirmations, focus, and emotional balance, that can guide you through any stage of life. They are simple, but they are powerful.

Use them consistently, and they will reshape the way you experience the world. When your thoughts, words, and actions align, you create a steady rhythm that carries you forward, even when the path is unclear.

So take what you have learned here and make it your own. Begin each day with appreciation, fill your thoughts with encouragement, and live with intention. Focus on what you want to create rather than what you fear. Believe in your ability to rise, adapt, and thrive. The more you practice, the more natural it becomes.

Positivity is not a single achievement; it is a way of life. It grows stronger every time you choose compassion over judgment, gratitude over complaint, and courage over hesitation. As you continue on your journey, remember this: the power to create lasting happiness has always been within you. You carry it wherever you go, in your thoughts, your choices, and your heart. When you choose to live from that place of clarity and peace, you are no longer just surviving. You are truly living.

ജ്ഷ